CHAMISA ROAD

 Random House/New York

CHAMISA ROAD

WITH...
PAUL &
MEREDITH

Doin' the dog in Taos

Paul.

thanks must surely go to...*david fenton*, for the classroom photo and lotsa
other stuff...*rich balagur*, for that neatso picture of the days of rage taken
from *RAT*...*steve shames*,of the *tribe* for that infamous photo of the guardsman
in chicago...*seed*, for the outasite statue of liberty creature...*steve rose*,
who we haven't seen for maybe years but took the picture of the lovely lady
with the tear gas mask on, and the one of the bippies all over the lovely
army jeep in washington deecee...*howie epstein*, of *lns*, who, if i remember right,
looks like clark kent and grabbed that l'il ole man pointing at paul's poem
just at the right moment...*fountain of light* from which we copped that photo
of the freaks hangin out at ye olde general store...*rini templeton*, for the
crucifixion drawing, the cambodian statues around the barkless lion days, and
the mesaincredible...

random house bob who smiles in just the right places and 11th floor susan who
runs around like crazy...
cori for the cover photos...
you other guys, you'll just have to know how important you are to the book and
to us.

PARTS OF THE WHOLE

a table of contents. table of fragments. multiplication tables. categories. yes, it's all there, right out front, see the figures, symbols, learn how to manipulate them, memorize each thing and it's place. maybe some of you have dug on the i ching. random fate, chance is the truth. but even the best edition of the i ching has a table of contents. how do you tie together the pieces of a book without separating them even more? we're trying to do as much as we can with this book. we don't want it to be just another book with a few hip gimmicks. we had a real hippy table of contents layed out **but who ca**res. it's hard. i guess the best would just be to run through the main streams of the river. like, we do want it to make "sense" and run, as streams do, from the mountains to the sea.

it starts out with some riffs to let you know what we used to be, who we used to were. what we were into and just history. after we historied we arrived out here. that makes sense. it's weird to start living in this land and we were weird about it. tell you more later. if you're into visions and ecstatic earth magic, new mexico sure will turn your head around. so will just about anyplace else, but we happened to be here. the earth visions melt into what you do every day. so we've written some about our down home life, as much as we can, which isn't very much. we used to ask people out here what they did every day, it seemed so boring. they never answered. now people ask us and we never can answer. and when we needed bread or some of that ol' bowels-of-the-monster excitement, we split for one coast or the other and we've written up that. and we've even tried to tell you/ figure out who we are. i don't remember what we decided the answer was/is, but it's not as important as figuring it out. we were going to put in some survival information but... and then at the end, we had a bunch of riffs about other **ends**, about Outside, about Politics, about Chicanos, about about a-bout. so we stuck them in there because they didn't fit anywhere else. okay?

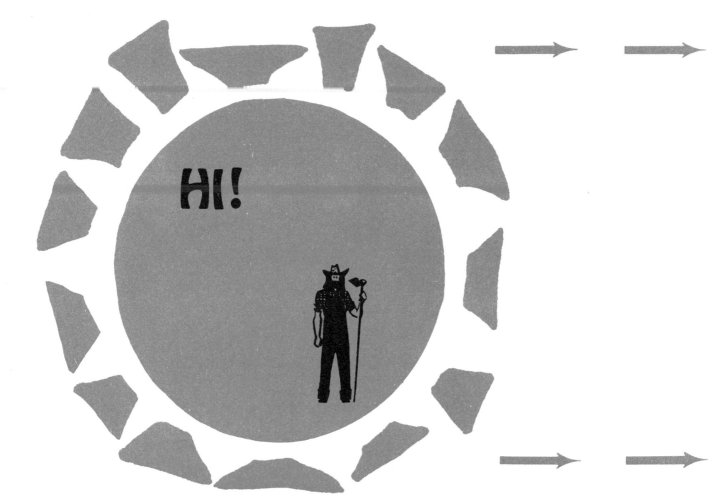

TO
BEGIN
RIFF:

OL' LEE...

DAVID TOOK THIS →

```
ALL the streets and ALL the schools are filled
with BROTHERS AND SISTERS who want
OUT!


who want something to DO!
who want someplace to GO!
who want to GROW
        and EXPAND
        and find LIFE prevailing over death
```

By different strokes of luck we all came to NEW MEXICO
    we've lived here (me and Trippy for almost two years)
    we've built houses, raised crops, watched the mountains
    and the mesas change, and stay the same

by SURPRISE we found people who love LIFE and are STRUGGLING
    to preserve it, to make it possible again, PEOPLE who
    know death as an inevitable visitation, not as a career

We want to SHOW our Brothers and Sisters what we've found (not tell nobody nothing!)

                              WORDS CAN BE USED TO CREATE -
                                  we can make a book of
                              IMPRESSIONS -
                                  a book to touch
                                  a book with space to breathe and be quiet
                                  a book alive with poetry of sage and smelling
                                      of juniper berries crushed underfoot
                                  a book that remembers Sangre de Cristo and
                                      Rio Grande-ee Gorge Bridge
                                  a book of being together by Doing together

We can make a book with living INFORMATION: about the people who call our New Place
HOME: what they EXPECT
                RESPECT
                ACCEPT. Information about a STRUGGLE to preserve LIFE in an unknown
peninsula called Northern New Mexico. Information about arriving naked and surviving
- about coming Prepared and Vanishing (or worse).

            A nice book - quiet, breathing, and alive -
            A HAPPY MANUAL that take its time -
            An introduction to LAST HOPE, to being TOGETHER

                        Don't miss it!

a book of much magic. i saw
a mountain today that wasn't
there yesterday and has al -
ways been there. my long
thin fingers stretched out.
leaping sagebrush. many
slender forest noises. incredible grayland.

"i'm a desperate man." hands
spread from wide-flung arms
and grip the edge of the table. "there's all this con-
sciousness around us and i've
got to turn people on to it.
man, we are just in the midst
of so much cosmic awareness
people got to dig it. sometimes it's just too much."
out of breath. "man i am
really desperate."

weird things knocked us out
of the assembly line and we
were stranded in liberation.
on both coasts and the glorious grey pittsburgh horizon,

gears shifted, valves overheated, rods were thrown, and minds rebuilt. we want people to dig on it. we want to reclaim the rainbow.

okay, these things come in scattered flashes so we won't try to straighten it out,
just get it all down as it hits.

maybe you don't know what this book is gonna be like. well, neither do we. the words
are all in a pile next to me now; stuffed into sentences, arranged into paragraphs and
pages, categorized into chapters. we've just started to lay it out, with all these
groovy designs and photos and colors and like that. and it's hard to get a feeling of
the whole thing yet, partially because it wasn't written in a pattern or block, and
mostly because there are so many other things happening now, which, i guess, is what
the book's about. there wasn't any reason for me to put in this rap, i just thought
it might bring us a little closer. hello.

P.S. 183 M.   Paul Steiner
Class 5-3   June 6, 1962

My Ambition

My mother always says that
in my father and his family's
veins "there runs ink instead of
blood." This saying holds true since
my father is an author, my aunt
is an artist, one of my uncles is the

editor of a newspaper, my other uncle
is in the advertising business, my
grandfather was an artist, and both
my cousins are adroit in drawing.

I hope to keep up the tradition
of writing in my family. When
I finish college, if I don't get draft-
ed, I will work for a newspaper as
a reporter. This would be in Colorado.

This is one of the things I
might be as a grown-up.

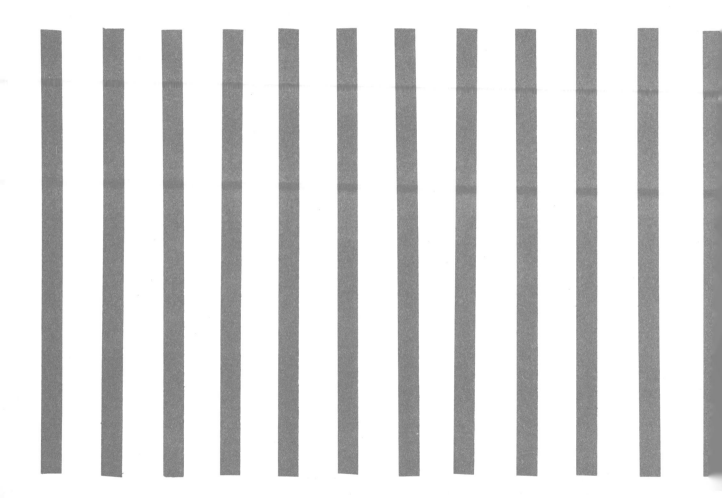

The Bronx High School of Science

75 WEST 205TH STREET　　　　　　BRONX, N.Y. 10468

DR. ALEXANDER TAFFEL
PRINCIPAL

TELEPHONE
295-0200

Date ___January 31, 1969___

To the Parents of ___Paul Steiner_____, Class ___4-22___ .

Your son/~~daughter~~ has been absent from school on ___32 regular___

school days this term_____ .

A large number of absences on a pupil's record may have an adverse
effect on his/~~her~~ opportunities at some time in the future.

I trust we will have your cooperation in reducing absences in the
future.

Very truly yours,

Giles M. Rae

Giles M. Rae　(S)
Discipline and Attendance

The Bronx High School of Science

75 WEST 205TH STREET BRONX, N.Y. 10468

DR. ALEXANDER TAFFEL
PRINCIPAL

ADM. ASS'TS

MR. A. BREINAN
MR. B. MANSON

Dear *Mr Steiner*,

An urgent situation concerning the behavior of
your child *Paul* has developed. It
is essential that you come to school to discuss this
matter and help find ways of guiding your child out
of this situation.

Please call my office Cy 5 0200 for an appointment.

Yours very truly,

very urgent !

Alexander Taffel

Alexander Taffel, Principal

The Bronx High School of Science

75 WEST 205TH STREET   BRONX, N.Y. 10468

DR. ALEXANDER TAFFEL
PRINCIPAL

TELEPHONE
295-0200

December 9, 1968

Mr. Stan Steiner
102 Greenwich Avenue
New York, N.Y. 10011

Dear Mr. Steiner:

I regret that it has become necessary to suspend your
son Paul as of Tuesday, December 10th. Please be in my
office on Tuesday, December 17th at 2 P.M. for a conference
to determine the future steps we may take together to make
possible his return to school. Until further notice your
child should be kept home during school hours.

Yours sincerely,

Alexander Taffel

Alexander Taffel
Principal

                              well,
                            see, we
                         had this scene
                      going in high school.
                    it was exciting back then,
                 but it's boring to write this a-
               bout it so don't expect too much. the
             man with his arm around me in the picture is
           an old friend from the six oh precinct and he's
         escorting me out of school. we got special treatment on a-
       ccount of our being Revolutionaries and bringing bunches of pub-
     licity to the alma mater. about three thousand light years ago we got
   an old mimeo machine and started one of the first high school underground
 newspapers. by my junior year i was suspended 22 times. merry worked in the
 dean's office and that's how we got to be such good pals. we used to run a-
 round inciting and like that and turning on in the bathrooms and getting all
 our friends to go demonstrating so they could get beaten up and radicalized.
 boy it sure was fun. we tried all the
 time to close down the school, but
 when the teachers went on strike naturally we climbed thru a window to open
                                  it up. the only thing i can say is that
                                  high school is a stone drag and i'm su-
 per glad that i got out when i did. that suspension notice you read was the
 last. when the truant officer came round to my old man, he signed a state-
 ment that read "whatever my son does to the bronx high school of science is
 fine with me" and that was the last i've had to do with it. as an afterthought
 i'd like to add that 50 people dropped out that year, which is only remark-
 able since no one ever had before in the school's history. well, i told you
 up front that you shouldn't expect too much.

the heading of the outline says: one - arrivals, reasons. yeah.
reasons.

i was maybe 4 or 5. i remember not being able to reach the table without tippytoes. don't remember much else except there were these
friends my parents had who had a house in The Country. i mean, they
lived there...that was before, i think, the days of the 5:45 to scars-
dale. it was in connecticut, and they had a cat named boots. there's
still a toobright color picture somewhere of me on the steps to the
house with boots in my lap. we used to go up there a lot, probly it
was only twice or 3 times, but as i said, it's about all i remember.
first thing i did in the house was find out where everything -
EVERYTHING - was so i could pretend i lived there. like if i had to
go to the bathroom i'd walk certainly in any given direction and maybe
end up in someone's bedroom and definitely forget about pissing, for a
while anyway.

second thing i'd do was run around, walk around the sidewalkless
streets saying wordlessly hi to all the other kids who (reflecting
now) stared and wondered who i was. even called the dogs by madeup
names - "hi rover, how does your paw feel today, sorry i forgot your
bone today fido." then we'd have to go home.

"why can't WE move to The Country? huh?"

"now sweetie, you know your father wouldn't like that, he hates mowing
lawns and things like that. and anyway he has nothing to do there, he
has to work in new york and that's where we have to live."

"I'LL mow the lawn ('what does mow the lawn mean?') and maybe daddy

could just work for a few more weeks and make enough money to buy a
house and then...then we wouldn't NEED any money."

they always tried not to laugh, i think   but the answer was always
the same. i always figured that it AT LEAST i could have a dog, it
would be ALMOST like living in The Country.

"daddy got bitten by a dog when he was young, and he couldn't stand
having one. maybe in a few years..."

it went on like that for years at least. "if we lived in The Country,
mommy, daddy wouldn't have to go to work." "but daddy has to go to
work, honey." "but daddy says he HATES to go to work. "you'll understand when you're older, dear."

well, shure enuf, i got older. and, in the process, learned all The
Reasons. i saw the rent bills, phone bills, bloomingdales' bills,
doctor bills, psychiatrist bills. i KNEW why daddy had to go to work.
but i still didn't understand. (still don't, not REALLY)

in between, though, i worked out The Plan. i'd start with turtles and
work my way through to a dog, and then...The Country. i won the first
goldfish at palisades amusement park, pitching pingpong balls into
their bowls. it died after a few days and i pretended to be heart-
broken enough to rate a turtle. i treated it like a dog.

"look mommy, i trained my turtle, he follows me." yeah. all the way
from one end of the dish to the other, if i held some of his food a
fraction of an inch from his nose. it took a long time for him to die
...and i really WAS upset this time. but it was taking a helluva long

time to get to the dog!

i never got past the hamster. he found his way into my father's bed
one night (i was maybe 13 by this time and well into Feeling Up Below
The Waist) and stopped the Plan dead. there were even salamanders en
route. they got out of their dish one day and the maid ("the cleaning
woman's coming today, meredith, so clean up your room.") found them
skeletally several months later. she quit right away, of course.
maybe not so much because of the sight of them, shriveled rightly they
were i hear, but at the thought of a 12-year-old GIRL having REPTILES
as pets.

then somehow i was fifteen years old and alive in gallup, new mexico.
me n my teenage lover living in a big red tent on the side of the hill
that housed the revivalist mission for the navajo reservation. "just
stop here, y'all, an drop off your bottles an save your souls." it
was a pretty awful summer. the tent had a way of becoming instant
oven the minute the sun rose, we were with paul's family & got caught
up in a lot of hassles, fought a lot, tried to learn to love balling &
hated it in the process, shit, it was HOT! but we found williecat
that summer in santa fe on our 6-month anniversary, we were together
if not Together, and...there was just something about the land...

then somehow i was sixteen years old and even more alive in san cristobal, new mexico, just a mile up the road from where i sit at this
very instant, living in a little cabin filled with sounds of the
stream out the window. me n my teenage lover sorta half wishing
school wouldn't start, new york didn't exist...but wondering too
what the hell we'd DO all year in a place like that.

we got back and got an apartment together, fought a lot, split up,

fought some more, and then paul split to new mexico. the letters were
real romantic but then the phone bill got unpayable so i flew out to
meet him.

john and rini were going to mexico for a month or so & asked us to
stay at their house while they were gone. a beautiful house, really,
almost at the edge of the Gorge & 2 great half-wild dogs & a comfy
bed...i hated it. lee came over one morning to bring us water and
i pounced on him. "what the hell do you DO all day?" he tried to explain, got to hand it to him, but...still i can't answer the same
stupid fucking question. snow all over the place, no vehicle, sick
from the water, panic letters from RAT & other city contacts...i'm
goin back to new york city, i do believe i've had enough.

months floated by. RAT unsaveable. everyone talkin about goin to The
Country, we had a truck, we went to the Country. blew into old san
cristobal, watched a lot of tv for a month or more, found trippy & lee
and we've hardly moved since.

the tv blew its mind out a few months ago. i've got my dog, my williecat, my front lawn needs no mowing, daddy doesn't go to work, and
here we are, me n my teenage lover, dreaming springdreams of food
growing and housebuilding. not to mention babies to come, not needing
to go to connecticut to pretend.

do we really NEED a reason?

i remember it now, yes, standing on some shore...sausalito, yes,
stranded. willie driven frantic smelling fish so near, so new to her
nose and not quite able to get at them, running on the rocks not quite
free, tied to a ball of string held by my hand.

*and we were talking about something, i remember only the feeling of
here we are, yes, in california, there must have been a reason for
coming this far, miserable.* so we were talking about rich hippies or
maybe dg's, the kind of people manson ripped off, i remember, yes,
saying something about their sound systems are better, their dope is
better, their bathrooms are better, their cars are better, so why
should we bother...? or something. mostly it was just what the hell
are we doing here so far from home standing alone in front of the
truck that probably won't make it back and not enough bread for gas
anyway, so we better develop a philosophy about it all quick to tell
the folks back home. make it all worthwhile. or something.

*i remember more now, a little, it was a feeling, the beginning of
the strong feeling,* that it is bullshit, maybe was not bullshit when
we spent so much time trying to create it and probably succeeding, but
now it certainly is bullshit and was, even then in sausalito. it was
that here we have brought to the sub-atmosphere all these beautiful
things, this music, this inhaling of weed, this balling in the bathtub, this mobility, and now, then, but now too, we have lost it. to
those other people. not the ones with the pasted-on sideburns. the
ones who are Really Into It.

it's not that heavy, really, yes, we still have our dope and new records all the time and now, even a bathtub (sears' best almost too

small for balling in). somehow, maybe it's only (only?) me but i feel
it can't be shared, not this way anyhow. not with Them. it's not
fair...but that's not what my head was full of at the top of the
page...

it was a memory. and now it's real, i can still feel writing all
those words and smiling over them with people who could have written
them too but maybe not the same way. *i can feel sitting there,*
not in the new office but on positively fourth street, especially
the day paul was on mike douglas...coming into the office first,
jeff rushing him to jerry's for the official tv hippie shirt, us bent
over the layout tables giggling/knowing we shared our smiles with
paul sweating somewhere in pancake makeup. and then maybe paul sambo
rushing in/out with - what was her name - yeah, mindy from the women's
commune in brooklyn. and bonny calling, wanting to know where's paul,
dutton called, it's cool, you can tell me. *the days/weeks fade together*...the day i decided & came in and told everybody, i'm going to
new mexico and they all knew what it meant and jeff took me into the
other room and told me he'd bet marvin and now was 5 bucks richer, and
then later maybe that day we balled to celebrate. and paul sambo
taking me into the other room to tell me he was glad, now he knew all
reason was not lost from the earth. and months later we sat in the
parking lot of the san francisco motor vehicles bureau waiting for his
road test talking about how we'd both dreamed we balled each other the
night before, and then kissing each other with smiles making the in-
spector mad.

and days after that, standing on the shore in sausalito.

but none of it says it. does it help to put here how jeff would look
around at maybe 4 or 5 am maybe speeding or giggling on coke or maybe
just wiped out on layout night, and say, wow! we've got the best
writers and dilists in the country right here at 5 am on east fourth
street! wow! and we'd all maybe tickle-tackle him to the floor for
being so bourgeoise, or maybe put "best writer in the country" next to
one of our names in the staffbox. drive him wild.

*but still this only draws flashing images into my brain...still doesn't
say...*

we believed it. we really, really believed it. we said it was ok if
all these hip capitalists were moving in, they could never really dig
grass or acid, it was cool. we said we wouldn't need guns, just look
at all the ads for runaways this week, it was cool. we said it was
funny that the fbi had rented the apartment across the street so they
could take pictures of us, it was cool. mostly we didn't talk about
shit like that. *it was all so fucking cool.*

             "WE ARE THE FUTURE!"
                        "THE POWER OF A MILLION SUNS..."
        "MY EYES MEET YOURS ON OUR STREET IN EVERY CITY..."
                     "BUILDING THE NEW AMIDST THE RUBBLE OF THE OLD..."

we believed it. we really did.

then one night we huddled around the new york times at carol's above
the office. someone named james rector was dead on telegraph avenue.
berkeley guns. and all of us stood at the narrow window magnetized by

the dark, waiting to hear the shots. and then carol got into bed and
melvin crawled in beside her. paul sambo crept off, alone. paul and
i went to 7th street. we didn't all sleep together that night. or
ever again.

and still, SMC asks nationwidely, where do we go from here? and meet
in anytown usa to argue about it. and the doorway lidsellers on telly
offer smack & speed. and carol's mother took her to puerto rico twice
to try to get her an abortion; finally she miscarried in her apartment
uptown. and jeff cut his hair to 'work down south.' and paulo is
gone to cuba to reclaim his body. and we need $50,000 for the land
we've been digging.

yeah, man, where do we go from here? WHERE?

positively NOT 4th street. knock on the door, no one's home. use the
credit card, phone no longer in service. put the stamps on the envel-
ope, address unknown. *vibes once spreading now turn inwards, i can't
find...*

I CAN'T FIND...

motor whirring, nothing more to say.

TAOS
TOWN LIMIT
ELEV. 6,950

the new jail

WE WROTE THIS ALMOST A YEAR AGO, SEEING IT ALL THROUGH SOOT-GRAY
EYES AND A SORT OF SENSE OF GUILT FOR BEING HERE AT ALL. IT WAS
HARD EVEN TO TYPE IT. WE HAVE REALLY GONE THROUGH SOME CHANGES.

At the Tastee Freeze on Santa Fe road you give your order through
a little window, they give you a number, you sit in your car and
wait for them to call it on the loudspeaker, you go to the window
and pick up your food and pay, then you go back and eat it in the
car. There is a new sign in the window, on top of the one for
rolled tacos. In black and gold lettering it reads "We Reserve
The Right To Refuse Service To Anyone We Consider a Health Men-
ace."

Just about anyone in Taos will tell you, you're nice, but those
hippies...The myth is very heavy and people refuse to give it up.
For a lot of them it's become a tactic of survival. The land can
not produce enough for your family, your children are moving to
Albuquerque, your TV is being repossessed, and goddamn those hippies.

The village we are living in, about 15 miles out of Taos, was vis-
ited by a State Police officer a few weeks ago. He told the chicano junior and senior high school kids in the valley that if they
wanted some exercise they should go into town and beat up some
longhairs. Some did. But then, it wasn't just that one cop;
their teachers had been encouraging them all winter to take part
in such extracurricular activities.

"Longhairs usually come from the big city and don't know that
water here is precious and hard to get. They see a stream and
wash their feet or dishes in it. Hey! That's our drinking water."

I WROTE THIS TODAY. THE SUN SHINES AND EVERYTHING'S COMING UP GREEN BUT WE'VE GOT THREE WEEKS BEFORE WE'VE GOT TO MOVE OUT OF THIS HOUSE AND THE BOOK HAS TO BE DONE BY THEN. SO I CAN'T GO OUT TO PLAY.

the sign's still there. they put in a new jukebox, too, and when you put in your quarter they look at you and if your hair's too you-know-what, they'll read numbers over and over, all through your songs. i don't think they've kicked anyone out yet...the local clean-cuts order small cokes and sit there for a few hours; stoned freaks come in and order two of everything. but the sign stays.

there's hardly anyone in taos who will tell you you're nice. they won't get close enough to find out...shooting range is about the usual distance. for many, like one of the managers of safeway who beat up some people in arroyo seco, the tactic of survival is the same as our parents.'

things got so heavy in the public schools here that some freaks set up their own. it's working.

it ain't only longhairs who left the beercans and potato chip wrappers in the streams to rot.

In a community as small as this one, a few freaks doing that while camping way upstream can do a lot of damage to local public relations. They did.

One of the co-chairwoman of the village's Community Action Project sat in her kitchen and said over coffee, "Sure, they paid their way. They have bough half a million dollars worth of land." She is a beautiful chicano mother who has tried to bring the people together. "But don't you see, that's exactly what the Anglos have always done, they take away our land."

Part of the thing she organized for the summer was a community school program. Most of the teenagers showed up for the first arts and crafts class. They discovered that the teacher was a hippie. The next week, they didn't go. One or two at a time, they are coming back.

"You know what those hippies did?" a farmer asks as if it was the crowning blow; "They built their toolshed in the middle of their field. Nobody builds a toolshed in the middle of a field."

The weekend we got to New Mexico, Tijerina and his Alianzistas were camping up north. They had just finished liberating a guest ranch run by the Presbyterian Church and had run the Governor of the State of New Mexico into hiding in the mountains by announcing that they were coming to serve a citizen's arrest warrent on him. They went to Los Alamos, where the laboratories of the Atomic Energy Commission are located, and announced that they wanted to arrest a scientist for crimes against the people. They didn't

out of the 30 **chicano** families in our valley, 2 or 3 make any
attempt at growing anything. at least trippy & lee & paul & i
are trying...and the communes have started growing enough to trade
with the co-op in tierra amarilla, and each other. does the land
belong to those who use it? or those who were here first?

that class didn't last very long. the cat who was teaching it
lives at reality construction co. now and last time we saw him
he was making a hothouse so they could grow strawberries and pep-
pers.

we just tore down that toolshed to make room for cucumbers. but
it was a pretty groovy toolshed.

know the names of any scientists, so they looked in the phone
book, found one, went to his house with a warrent, and discovered
he wasn't home. So they burned a National Forest sign and cut
some fences to symbolically reclaim their land. Then they all
got put in jail.

We bought a TV this week. None of our friends will talk to us.
But it's almost worth it. The news is beautiful. They announce
"and here is Joe Shmoe in Washington" and you sit there for five
minutes watching a blank screen. Then the announcer comes back
and pretends nothing happened and you can actually see him blush-
ing. Then, during the sports news, Joe Shmoe appears and starts
talking about what's happening in Washington.

In this valley where we live there is a chicano farmer-poet-wood-
carver-handyman who, when in the right mood, can orate for hours
on end about life and death and Nixon and Indians and the Church
and the people and the land and anything else with a 300-year-old
Castilian accent and one of those boys' camouflage cowboy hats
that you get for 98 cents in an army-navy store cocked to one
side of his head. After delivering the most beautiful philoso-
phical rap you've ever heard, he ends up saying, "but I'm just a
dumb Mexican."

The TV is sort of typical of the State. One day they lost the
movie they were supposed to show. The commercials always come on
at the wrong time and the sound is never synched to the film. The
whole thing comes off like an amateur talent show. In a way, so
does everything else. People play their roles with a little grin.
They can be totally immersed in something and still you can feel

tijerina's still in jail. that was a year ago. the sign's been
replaced. what more can i say?

the tv broke and we just had it fixed about a week ago. what's
happening in washington now is a few hundred thousand angry kids
who can't believe THAT could happen in OHIO. or cambodia, for
that matter.

this guy has spent most of his time since then putting down hippies and threatening to shoot any dog that comes near his land.
his turkey eggs were getting stolen and he said, "I think it's
that Steiner dog." his raps ain't so beautiful any more.

nobody's grinning. it's all pretty serious all of a sudden.

that underneath they are just waiting for the curtain to fall.
Then they'll get involved in something else. When you are hip to
yourself you can play the game with immunity.

We need a round table for the kitchen. Too much empty space, it's
not warm enough to be the center of the house as kitchens are out
here. A rug for the living room. A work bench, tool rack, and
some other things to fill up the study. The carpet is in Mexico,
also dishes and trinkets; the rest can be made from odds and ends
lying around in back. Except the round table. Too complicated
for me to figure out.

In the morning Merry'll scrub the kitchen floor and I'll take the
garbage up to the dump. Maybe our refrigerator will be ready.
That would be nice. Maybe Stan will get here with Nashville Skyline. That would really be nice. The thunder is the loudest I've
ever heard, it's so dark and wet you can't even see the starts
except in brilliant flashes of desert lightining. Merry lying in
bed singing Tim Hardin. The rain comes and goes in muddy torrents.
It is healing rain. The coffee is thick and hot. Willie Kitten
is curled on the windowsill washing herself. Even she's less
neurotic than she was in New York. Once we've turned this house
into our home, what happens? Once it has rugs, round tables, and
a record player, where do we go? Well, it'll be a month or six
weeks before we've finished. That's a long time. And if we decide to move around we'll still have a home. We'll also have to
get some paint and plaster in town tomorrow. If the road's not
washed out. If it is, there's plenty of things to do anyhow.

A bunch of days have passed and I just noticed that this page is

and nobody's immune.

we got all that stuff. the table is outasite. so's the rug.
mexico was a depressing drag. and the raps around the kitchen
table mostly turned into hot arguments about whether or not we
"deserve" to be here and the shade of our skin.

women's libbies, are you listening? just for the record, paul's
washed the kitchen floor, and the dishes, as many times as i have.

where we went was san francisco, with trippy & lee, for about a
month. when we came back, we didn't have a home. some of the
local kids broke in and stole some stuff, shat on the floor,
rubbed shoe polish into the rugs, and destroyed the windows. so
we found another house right on the road and made sure when we
went to nyc there were people staying here.

still in the typewriter. It doesn't really matter, I'm still wearing my US Keds and the same pants. The world's still here. Merry's feeling sort of down and is still lying in bed.

We got a refrigerator! Started painting, putting in windows and screens, building things. Stan brought Nashville Skyline and gave his blessings on our home. He also indirectly inspired both of us to do up some novels. It's still raining.

Rumors are reaching us of two hundred thousand ripped-up draft cards, the SDS-PL split, the heavy paranoia on the Lower East Side, and a fairy riot in the Village. Right on. Thinking of New York brings back all kinds of possible images and energy flashes. But not from hip energy which had bursts (Fillmore, high schools, the first Be-In) because hip energy in New York was mostly from speed. The possibilities in the City are for media and growth. There are a lot of chicks on the Upper West and East Side who can be turned on by a good hippie fuck, etc. There is not enough space for living. Action in New York becomes meaningless and frustrating after a while. It's a good place to turn people on but there isn't anywhere for them to go when they're turned on.

Stan told us that all the hitchhikers he saw were heading for New Mexico. Time magazine said that there will be ten thousand in Taos this **summer** . Baby, please don't come.

First of all, there are a lot of good people out here. We are trying to create space for the community, but we are just barely getting enough for ourselves. It takes time. If more people come out, especially if they're just floating around, we are all going to get kicked out. It was very hot here until a couple of

thinking back, lying in bed was about all i could find to do.
it's taken this long to get over city/action mentality.

did 40 pages of a novel. it sucks.

rumors are reaching us now of sds gone 'underground' with most
of them either in jail or on the way, no one left of the lower
east side, and gay liberation yet another category to fit yourself into. new york is a good place to turn people on...to scag
and the politics of death.

ditto.

weeks ago, and it's bound to get worse before it gets better.
There are people who have been here for two or three years and
they are just beginning to have a relationship with the community.

The main problem began with the fact that most of the freaks who
came out did not realize where they were going. This is not the
mother country. It's the colony. The chicanos don't need to
have their minds blown by clothes, hair, obscenities, and other
city/survival/identification numbers. They have a culture which
is not the suburban Amerikan vulture kulture. As a matter of
survival in what is a classic colonial situation, the chicano culture has developed very strict family structures and very repres-
sed sexual morality. Public nudity and balling and media myth-
ology of "free love" resulted in cultural hostility and then the
rape of several hip chicks. In the city it is cool, even pref-
erable, because of the total life anonymity and social structure,
to relate to people through the hip revolutionary myth. Out here
it is necessary to relate as people. The majority of the popu-
lation are our potential brothers, not parents. Right now, however,
we are still gringos.

There is much you can do before you come out here. Find out why
the National Parks are hated, find out about Kit Carson's Indian
massacres, learn about the Hispano and Indian cultures. The fact
that you have a poster of Geronimo on your wall and always root
for the Indians does not mean you understand what New Mexico is
all about. Get El Grito del Norte and know the struggle out here.
By the time you know enough to survive, I hope we will be ready
to open our home to you. If you come out now, it's all over.

I'm really sorry this is so harsh, but we all made mistakes along

it's gotten worse...and worse, and still hasn't begun to get better.

i think that a lot of the chicanos could use a good mind-fuck. not
to mention a good body-fuck. "obscenities?" jesus. all my
clothes have been divided into san cristobal clothes, taos clothes,
santa fe clothes, and ny/san fran clothes. all those years fight-
ing in high school against clothing regulations...and now i make
my own.

fuck that gringo shit.

the best thing you can do before you come out here is think about
someplace else to go and then go there. if you get el grito,
you'll find out that the "vanguard" on the chicano "liberation"
movement is relating to the "people" by writing article after
article setting up freaks as the enemy. THAT'S the struggle out
here.

the way and if the hip community and our alternative way of life
is to survive, we can't make the same mistakes twice. If we are
wiped out now, we'll grow again because we are the future but I'd
rather not get wiped out anyhow.

if we are wiped out now, it'll be with the rest of the planet.
there might not be a future. which, i guess, is the whole point

brothers, sisters,

and others:

we've been mostly out here in new mexico for about six months now.
which is not very long considering the mountain on my left and the
desert on my right, but it's a long time for me, having learned as
much in six months as in eleven years of school. anyhow things are
settling in and the time has come for me to write this to you.

RAT, which can occasionally be gotten in santa fe, seems to have death
in its veins. that was predictable. on our last stay in the big city
we tried to get it to move, to open itself up, to live, but it refused.
the point of revolution, or of life (which is revolution),is change.
the underground press is incapable of it and has become pablum.

about two months ago, on our way back from a short trip to san francisco, i started an article which said something like "we are awaiting
the sunburst which will be the rebirth of the revolution," etc. i am
beginning to get impatient. a couple of days ago, lee and i took some
acid, and rode my motorcycle down a deserted dirt road into a little
canyon and watched the seasons change. and i have smoked almost half
a pack of camels in writing this already because i can't seem to say
what i need to say. winter is sliding fast into this valley and
everything is slowing, getting ready for the hibernation pace. the
mind, which had little exercise in the physical spirit of summer, be-
gins to agonize. what the fuck are you people doing?

hey you guys...you don't know what yer missin. us vs you - honeygold aspens pouring
down sunrich mountains - vs transplanted indignation running a muck in the streets of
pigtown usa. not to mention quiet people knowing it's gonna happen/is happening - vs
screaming buttonwearers determined to know just how. not to mention do you really
WANT chicago/nyc/boston/detriot? isn't that more like what THEY deserve?

ah, you should see the land now. it smiles serenely in the face of your frenzy and
knows so much of our love. every-
thing is a different color/texture/
smell/beauty every day. the mountains are sculpted by steadysure
fingers; the sky just floats on its
back, not bothering to watch.

yesterday afternoon, on the way
back from santa fe in our funky ole
truck, i drank a can of Hamm's
("born in the land of sky blue wa-
ters," made in chicago) and watched
the setting sun. about ten miles
up, the highway disappears into
the cliffs of the rio grande gorge
and i decided to try to describe it
in words which is very hard because
t's a total trip and not at all linear. the land swoops in front of you mostly
rown spotted with green. for an hour or two before that ball of fire goes out ev-
rything becomes so crystal clear that it's hard for your mind to handle it. the
anyons with their pale burning sharp red walls and blue shadows are completely flat
n top and the brown grass disappears. the green spots, which are called pinon trees
ut look more like strung-out bushes, grow out of the crevices in the stone. by the

time i got that far in my description we had gone through velarde,
with its fruit stands and gas stations, and entered the gateway of the
gorge. from there the road winds back and forth and up and down for
about 30 miles which i will not even try to describe.

* *

it was the first time last nite that we watched it all happen the way
amerika does...on teevee...and it seemed perhaps only more absurd to
us than to Them. did all those people really follow sds blindly down
its deadend road...or was it wide-awake death-wish? thought We were
past watchin parkin meters by now. the broken bank windows were about
as new as daley's speech.

i'll confess, it's not really enough here either. sometimes we spend
days/nights stumbling in the loveliness, trying to find something to
DO. sometimes we watch every show, one after another, eating tv din-
ners and feeling ashamed. wavering amidst cityconsciousness. missing
the nightly nod-outs on st. marx. wondering if we're affecting anything outside. feeling it happen inside.

and then trippy & lee come & we maybe get stoned or talk about silk-
screening or making jam & maybe do it.

and then once in awhile something happens to remind us that we're
something to come home to.

a week or two ago i was sitting in a coffeeshop in town and this cat
with real short hair and a moustache was sitting one seat away. a
chicano greaser came in and sat between us. he was wearing a "hawaii"

t-shirt and looked like most people did 15 years ago which is the way
the local kids look. the cat with the moustache asked him how come
there were so many young people in this little town. the greaser said
oh, you mean the hippie trash, i guess they like it here. i was just
flashing on the fact that it was until we got here that it was the
mexican trash, when hawaii sneered at me, got up, and walked out. the
cat with the moustache moved over and told me he'd just gotten back
from viet nam and had spent his 30 day leave in l.a. trying to find
some good people to talk to and he was on his way up to fort carson in
colorado to do 14 more months and he happened to stop in taos and he
couldn't figure out why there were so many good people in this town
with 5 gas stations and 2 hardware stores. so i started to explain it
and he ended up spending his last 3 days with us. we took him around
the northern half of the state and got into some heavy raps about nam
and survival and revolution and i don't really know how to begin to
put it onto this piece of paper...one flash of light in the night
means it's all over. lee said it made him feel like the hip revolution is a birthday party.

just yesterday we got a letter from fort carson. he says, "dig on
this, there is an establishment-sponsored coffee house on post. It's
called the "Inscape Coffee House" and is replete with black light,
peace signs, the zig-zag man, "Better Living Through Chemistry" pos-
ters, heavy head music, folk singing groups weekly and is all brought
to you by the local protestant chaplain."

* *

last night was the first time in my life i've been outa da city for
the first snow of the year. when paul came and said look out the win-

dow!, i never even considered the possibility. because 1) it doesn't
snow in early october 2) the weatherman didn't say it would and 3)
when the first snow comes you can tell by listening for sounds of snow
chains in the street and snow shovels scraping the sidewalk. well,
the road outside the window was unusable and i haven't seen a real
sidewalk for 6 months.

hours before that, we'd watched the third night of the Days of Rage in
chi, hearing of pigs with broken necks & smashed faces. still feeling
how wrong/worthless but nonetheless being reminded of country joe's
"let's hear it for the good guys! YAAAAAAAY! let's hear it for the
bad guys!   BOOOOOOO!" so i threw the i ching to try to know if being
a good guy in da country is good enough.

'hexagram 49: revolution. on your own day,
              you are believed.
              Supreme success,
              Furthering through perseverance.
              Remorse disappears.

'the first thing to be considered is our inner attitude toward the new
condition that will inevitably come. We have to go out and meet it...
only in this way can it be prepared for.'

is that the new condition? or living without need of jobs, school,
schedules, or The Struggle? living with the land in the ying-yang
of cybernetic revolution.

'One who is central and correct is able to bring out all the good of
such a revolution. Therefore it is said of this line: "The great man

changes like a tiger."'

yeah, you can go through changes on michigan avenue - like a caged
tiger. enraged and helpless. get caught between the bars.

there's not much more to say. i've never before felt myself in a position to say this, but...i really feel that you're wrong. the city is
wrong. synthetic energy is wrong. simulated revolt is wrong. the
land - and the people who can learn to dig it in their own ways - are
on the way.

go and join us.

meredith & Paul

DOWN HOME VIDA

"and what for you?"
"just the mail, elmira, and" - oh god - selective service system -
shit - what... (Dear Sir, you requested a CO form and we never...) -
"a dollar of gas please."

"pump ran out on us this morning, paul seagull got some and now i just
can't -"

can i make it to town? missing dust cap on front axle, who knows how
much gas -

"thanks elmira, see you later."

god! dig that mesa - so many colors, god! so much - shit! what's
that goddamn NOISE? is the whole front wheel loose? did paul fix it
wrong? enough gas? well turn off the engine & roll into hondo, car-
eening around that scary curve a little ice on the road WHY didn't
paul put the chains on?! must be goin 70 and in this ole -

a crowd with its thumbs out - how long is their - yeah, freaks, roll
to a halt, get in everybody.

"we're going to taos."
yeah. where else? "been around here long?"

"no, we just got here from berkeley a few days ago, been up at morn-
ingstar but it's heavy up there, don't know how much..."

it's only WINTER! hordes already...what about this SUMMER?! (the new
jail, no windows, they're ready...)

..."longer we can stay there, do you know of any..."

yeah. houses for free, come to Da Cuntry & hop in the sack with the
rest of the pioneers, split the city for new mex, get your head together, live for free, the natives are friendly -

..."houses we can live in? i heard there were lots of abandoned ado-
bes..."

adobe. a genuine OUTWEST word. 3 points, brother.

"try the real estate agents. you planning to stay?"

"oh yeah, really dig the country, the city's so uptight, man, death
trip, man. yeah, gotta. gotta stay. gotta find a place."

"you been out here long?"

"3 years, on and off, yeah."

"WOW!" you must have a - place - and...EVERYTHING!"

well now i'm instantly transformed into this sorta real downhome together chick who's been roughing it out here 3 whole years, way ahead of
the times a real...

"you live in a commune?"

angelic smile. "no, nothing that formal."

"oh. WOW."

...condcooonding bitch pulling the supercilious trip, baby don't come,
maybe next week we got an incredible losing streak in the makin...

drop em on the plaza with directions to the food stamp place - what
right do these FOREIGNERS have comin in here 3 days and already eatin
up the TAXPAYERS' money?!!!!!! fuckin...

do the bank, park across the street can't risk that parking lot, i'm
not in control the truck is on tracks like in those go-karts-pay-yer-
money-&-pretend-yer-drivin while the man sits in the booth & steers
you around the circle - always have this feeling coming into town but
not usually this strong - sense of eminent disaster - but nothin i can
do. do the food stamps meet phillip who shows me weird shoes just in
from persia or somewhere with curly tops, leave the office, turn the
key, truck don't say boo. yeah. doesn't even surprise me that two
minutes ago it was fine and now - NOTHING. only hope this is the
worst of it. paul seagull's jeep parked next to mine, he's nowhere in
sight, oh well can always wait for him to come back & get a ride home
& come back later maybe for the truck.

but phillip comes out & offers to give us a push, soon there are 15
freaks pushin & the truck gives a mighty roar & i'm off to miller's
for the dust cap. leave the engine running just in case. time to go
to the doctor...i think. i mean i know there are other things i gotta
do now that i'm here IN TOWN but shit i can't hardly see straight
there's a tragedy in the cloud above me & it just - might - rain...

i got LOST! yeah - lost in this tiny honkytown with hardly enough

streets for all the souped-up 53 oldsmobiles, and i can't find my goddam way, keep goin round & round the plaza, gotta get to the clinic,
gotta get to the...finally make the decision, appointment at 2:30 dunno what time it is but just can't think any more...*(safeway)*...maybe
later...

so i've made the decision, waiting to make the turn, i know which way
to go, i've got a DIRECTION and the truck stalls, try to start it. NO.
ok. i take the keys & my jacket & go for a walk. *(the doctor! 2:30!
what time*...) walkin around the plaza in circles, sorta lookin for
paul seagull, lookin for a clock in some window, no go, can't - CAN'T
go in or ask someone and it must be near 2:30 so i got to paul's jeep
- i've got an ANSWER! - to leave a note to pick me up at the clinic ⊾
but who knows if paul will ever get it - see some freaks in a shiny
new 4-wheel driver, they look like they can handle it all, ask them to
give me a push...

"can you do me a favor? i..."

"sure!!! anything!!! what do you need?"

but then here comes paul - "never mind, problem solved -"

"oh, paul seagull! yeah, he'll take care of you."

paul's hung up with some drunk indian who seems to want to find a band
for his son's wedding..."guitars, lotsa guitars, and drums! lotsa
drums..."

paul keeps tryin to find out where, when...but it's obvious to me, anyway, the cat just wants some bread...

"is that your wife?"

"no, she's a good friend."

"she sure is pretty. god, she's pretty. wish i..."

(paul, come ON! can't you see the cat just wants...)

"well i gotta do some business, man, later..."

the indian realizes it's now or never & sticks out his hand, palm up
...paul with 4 bucks to his name gives him a handful of change & we
start to get into his jeep to get to my truck & up comes DANIEL! with
the incredible magic eyes...

"hi paul, goin south?"

"i'll take you to the general store, daniel."

"no, i just wanna go to safeway..."

(safeway's only a block away! what the fuck...)

so we climb into the jeep all on top of each other & drive to my truck
& we're blockin traffic & a cop drives by & suddenly there's 10 mostly
drunk indians standing around & suddenly each of them has one hand on
me and one in the engine...paul dashes off down the street..."gotta
find a wrench somewhere..." i'm sittin in the engine scraping shit

off the battery & this young indian cat is telling me...

"i've got problems, you know? but it's cool, i KNOW i got problems,
but they're TERRIBLE problems, do you think you could..."

"i've got to do this, man, later..."

paul comes back with some straight cat whose wrench it is & suddenly
there's ten or twenty indians standing around all claiming to be re-
lated to little joe indian.

"i'm little joe's uncle." "i'm little joe's brother." "i'm little
joe's cousin."

and each time they say it, the young guy next to me grabs my arm &
says "little joe is my father." so i say yeah? and he says, "no,
little joe is my uncle." it's too much. daniel is makin magic eyes
at me but bein of no help atall, says he lost his best pipe...suddenly
paul's sayin we'll push it & i say should i try to turn it on first &
he says no & suddenly there's ten drunk indians in front & ten in back
and they're all pushin in different directions & i'm tryin to find out
where they're pushin me to & i decide, "RUN, TRUCK!" & turn the key &
shure enuf...BRUMM!

one indian still has his arm on my arm & i give paul an SOS look & he
says, "put it in gear, man, and GO!" so i do, spinning off drunk indians as i go, and rush to the clinic.

the chick at the desk can't find my fucking card. "are you SURE
you've been here before? are you SURE you've paid your bills?" she
won't even tell me what time it is, am i late? she doesn't even be-

lieve i exist. "you can't see dr. rose till i find your card." finally she lets me fill out a new one.

dr. rose is on the phone to the husband of someone who just tried to
kill herself or something & he's got to sew her legs back on. "BOTH
legs, huh? well, make the appointment for 4:30, i'll operate at 5."
then he calls the nurse. "have a lot of blood ready, i don't know if
i'll use it or not but have it ready. a lot of blood."

go outside to find my truck encircled by cars, two of them with people
inside but they won't move, takes me a half hour to get outa the parking lot, go to safeway, meet phillip, yeah, i'll drive you to san
cristobal, get followed around inside by sammy the deafmute clerk
who's waiting for me to steal something so i do & he grunts but does
nothing. WHAAAAAT????

phillip & i are on the way out of town, he's telling me about how he &
a friend took acid & went to the hot springs at 4 ayem, i'm thinkin
about easy rider, we're coming up to these 2 pickups parked right on
the highway, there are 2 chicano cats talkin & drinkin, i have to go
around them.

"no, i never went to the hot springs but i saw what they look like in
..."

BLAM! we hear sounds just like gunshots, **we** both duck & come up shak-
ing...look back, there's smoke rising from one of the pickups...

..."easy rider." shit! paranoia or...

there was more, too. but i can't go on. i mean, all in ONE DAY...

it's really impressive and hopefull to see a beautiful place built by freaks and the houses up there are out of sight. i felt like i was standing on liberated land, land where anything is possible. a place where you can feel the freedom to DO IT. It's so much more open than it is in this valley, living on land like that is bound to open you up and inspire your body every time you look up.

it was pretty cold and it started getting dark so we went back to pat and
will's and ate dinner and froze in the back of the pick-up through the
mountains and to our valley. as it is right now, we may have found some
land up there, we'll probably find out tomorrow. even if we don't get it,
it's nice to know it exists. cross your fingers.

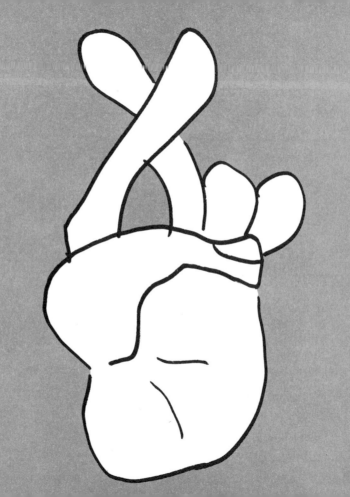

on one day there was a trail and i followed it. the sun came with me
to light my way and keep me warm. this trail was just wandering
around, but i wasn't in any rush to learn its secret. i munched on my
romantic hiking raisins whenever i remembered, and i cut a sweet but
short aspen walking stick with a hook at the end. i contented myself
with the realization that if deershit got wrinkled it would look like
raisins and might taste good too. but none of the deershit i passed
was wrinkled so i didn't have a chance to prove or disprove my hypo-
thesis. it didn't take as long to think as it just did to write, it
might have just been a flash. the trail went farther than i did, because i got tired and came back.

* *

today we cleaned up the house and put all our scraps of writing in a
pile and then went through it and sorted them and it really felt good
and it was a whole lot more than we thought we'd done and we got happy
because this is going to be an outasite book.

* *

i want to writ somethin down here but can't seem ta. dunno wha. got
me happy home yeah got me hoppy Woman yeah got me hippy mountain range
so strange. d'you really want t hear anymore. whot candy say????????
how much for dose preety teeties. maybe you would like t writ this
buke stead a me (iIMe). hah. i most warm - it's bounding to arrive
much moor seriose. hah, heh, hoh, how (got it) to trace a shaky path
(beat a bush?) a way from the Heavies. hooah. whee.

the beast whey may be not t look read at it. a nanser undoubted for tee hip-harted. may be yoost a kweek looky in de pixtoors. den we go back to bed an make duh orgasm.

* *

new mexico is a state of deserts and mountains and towns, mostly desert towns and mountain towns, even more mostly desert villages and mountain villages. there is albuquerque with 250,000 people (about 1/4 of the total pop) but albuquerque is too strange to include as part of the state or anything else. santa fe is populated by retired philanthropists, ex-colonels, state government bureaucrats, and their servants. it's the Cultural Center. you can buy almost any Culture you want there.

* *

i was just wishing we had a car so i could drive into town (it's a real trip to drive our old truck and you have to be in the mood, you can't just go somewhere in it), but it's past midnite and there probably isn't any place open except the **shamroc**k **truc**k **stop**and you take your life into your hands getting coffee there. it's at time like this that i **miss** the big city. can't wait to get busted outside gem's spa again. i haven't had an **egg** cream in over six months. i made blintzes the other night and it was probably the first time they were ever inside the state line. life's rough. i really do miss it, somehow i and we have got to do a thing that doesn't start and end in one place, country or city.

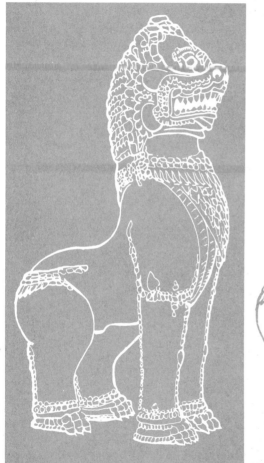  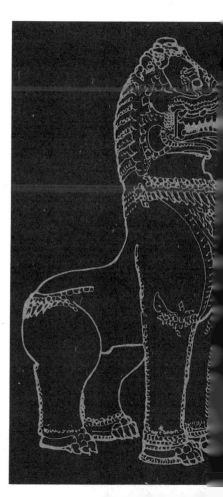

some days the lions don't even bark.
i think i've been having a general
lot of barkless lion days. peeking
into dreaded spedded crises. charming the rocks. guess some barking
must have been done. in the name of
some undoubted lord. if the frost
don't come soon it may not come at
all, or it may come later. much to
wait for.

a little breeze chirps by. rustling, sweet-touching my face. eyes
closed upwards sun-blessed. minty sharp tongued sage-smell flicks its
tail under my nose. wind-sun-sage rhythms, fingertips on my heart,
slowing, growing, knowing. plucking bits of pinon bark from my hair,
burrs from my socks and jeans. it can really be nice out here. a
sound, i look up. ticking. a clock in the sun-face. a clock of fire.
what time is it? shit, forgot my glasses, can't tell the time. maybe i'm lucky, maybe it's one minute before the apocalypse. next time
i have a vision hope i bring my glasses.

songs of tomorrow/ just lookin for a taste of

your greenery/ makin pretty little sagebrush

smiles run down yer spine/ pockets of yer

sun and they don't seem to shine on me/

that old jar by the door?/ askin for

a little more/ don't worry bout

the store/ not much time left

to score/ can't play my an-

cient clausewitz gone all

t hell.

just to say, i'm me,

and seeing as i most

probly will be for some

time to come, me is all i

have to offer.

my history has come to pass/ quetzalcoatl
shines in open adoration/ the new way/
there is a hewn oak door alone in the
orangeness of the mesa and the purple
sunbeam filters thru the keyhole/ no
shadows will be sold/ the stranger in
silver calls the hand and the cards are
turned over/ a moment of silence for
the gambling man.

```
meredith of the brite white gleemy sheen
how ravaging is yer wave of hair
black spread
            wide eyed
                      glory squeak
tender mount
wing spanned delight
thunder maid sweet toned taste
honey belly
            tracks
                    tack
                         back
                            mate of
fire juices deluging all out an into
dawn slides thru sleeped lids
singing fields shouting
and jumpin an hal
                  le
                    lu
                       yah
from mellow thinned altogether
```

the killer arose before dawn. the people gathered in the town square.
the men huddled on the steps of the church. the women shivered and
babbled on the benches. during the night the hands of the clock on
the steeple had vanished. the sun tipped the horizon. a scream inside the church. the sun turned black. the men rushed inside. from
the crucifix above the altar, blood was dripping.

scag flames singe the souls of brothers and sisters. speed demons
dance bodies into dust.

creeping thru the desert, speeding down the freeway, bursting chaotic
exhaustion across the bay bridge, as kerouac said, can't go no further,
this is the end. the hills of missouri, illinois corn, saint louie,
great gray highway, pittsburgh, merging traffic, stretching out forever, all those lives, all those scenes.

cross the continent looking for a reason. maybe i had to be on the
mesa to learn there is no reason. there can be none. the sun rises
and there is snow on the ground. for the first time. the clouds are
not cumulus or nimbus, they are beautiful. the sun is not a small
star, it is glorious orange. in the morning it shines on your new
body. power to the people.

walking down a road the other day, i looked out at this planet, and
saw where it curved around. i could see mountains but i couldn't see
their bases, they started past the horizon. a rush of planetude. a
new connection with this ball of earth. me sittin here here watching
the roundness, another speck on this mountain and all that. this rap
is either getting closer or further from the point i'm trying to make,
i don't know. the earth is living, it is life. and we're looking for
some way to plug in, to join ourselves with the flow of life. i got a
rush of making that connection up on the mountain there. and the land
we're gonna get now, it's got that feeling. the air is cool and moist
smelling, each tree twists and loops its own rhythm or shoots straight
up into the waiting sky, the sage needs only to be asked gently to
spark the wind with its tingling taste. merry could feel the water
flowing below the surface with her hands. sitting on a tuft of long
grasses, my fingers are playing around with the earth next to me,
scooping it up, filtering out little pebbles of quartz and things,
bits of bark and twigs, pine needles, feeling the dampness underneath.
so many trips going on in every inch. sliding down the snow into one
of the canyons. fifty or a hundred feet down to the bottom and the
ponderosa pines shoot twice as high out and past the top. soft bed of
fallen needles and confused cactus waiting flashy spring flowers. the
gorge widens and the sides climb higher and steeper thru layers of
adobe and even fiery sandstone. on the other side of the arroyo i
crossed two deer trails and i'm not a vegetarian.

sleepy hair
tangles over
sunrise-warm cheeks

JORNADAS

titled:
almost on our way
to
glorious
golden
california.
to
friendly faces
to
cliff-shadowed
beaches
to
rainbow bands
of long-haired
lunatic
lovers

   the story says people come to the bay area to flip out.
   we journeyed from new mexico in our old panel truck and were
just about wiped out in the mojave desert when we picked up two dudes
in cowboy hats and ankle-short skin tight chinos who knew all about
cars, having totaled five on their way from chicago to l.a. looking
for jobs. outside of fresno we did the a&w root beer thing and an old
lady in a broken down convertible next to us played with a baby ba-
boon wearing pink undies. no one blinked. we left southern california
and sped over the bay bridge into the fog, ending up in a mansion by
the ocean. took showers and went to the haight to pick up some papers
and see what was happening.
   a cat and a chick standing on the corner, both about thir-
teen. "i don't care if you're six months gone, i've got 104°." we split.

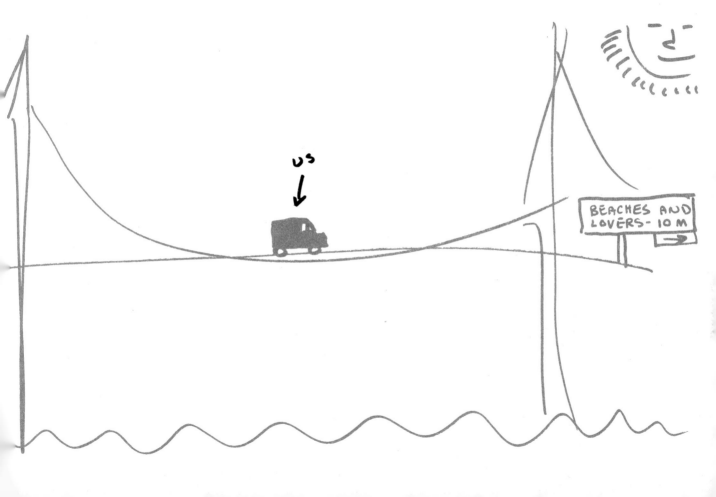

what a feelin, t fly so fast &
high & know we was goin directly
in the wrong direction and not
even time to remember when suddenly we start goin down through
a cloud 22,000 feet thick and
it's AAAAUUUGH! NEW YAWK! "paul!
there's no colors!"

an standin there at the airport,
lookin around - "paul! how did
this happen?" a flash of the all-
overinside new mex calm disinte-
grating into that ole bigcity panic and a clear choice: harden
and survive or maintain that
sweet innocent gentle we know we
was all born with and be DROWNED
in the sea of angry uglies running WHERE? round these parts, ya
can't just swim. ya gotta jump
aboard someone else's high-power-
ed speedboat and be whisked to
places you never wanted to be.

i'm sittin here sayin this to ya
from a paper-thin apartment they
got for the view. "we moved, wait
till you see the view!" and all

i can see is 4 con ed smokestacks and a lot
of cars crawlin up first ave, ready to attack my brain. keep tryin to see that mesa,
oh! WHERE'S MY MESA? all brown and sometimes gray-green except at sundown all incredible orange with mountains 150 miles
away sayin, "we'll always be here."

an every time i pass a phone i jump inside
& dial all kindsa numeros an hold my breath
& say, "trippy? lee? are you...is it?" an
they say, "it's all here, meredith. can
you get back for thanksgiving?"

an lordy, the people here...an the rules. so many rules! how kin ya live yer life
if ya hafta keep givin the bus an extra nickel or dime because they gotta rule about
no change given by driver an all the stores around the bus stop have signs saying no
change given for bus an if ya put the whole quarter i ya won't have enough left to git
home later and ya know if ya ask anyone fer change they'll all be hordin nickels and
dimes like they was friends?!

how kin ya be at peace if ya know that the sun
gets up an hour or two before it makes it throug
the smog strong enough to smile at you and gets
lost an hour or two before it really sinks under
the filthy hudson?!

how kin ya find love when ya gotta worry allthe-
time about DYIN?!

gotta get out. i kin feel myself startin again to wait telephones & elec-
tric orangejuicemakers & 2 bathrooms & plastic dresses & cleaning ladies &
peppridge farm bread & taxicabs. what else is there to want here?

gotta get out. been smokin more than ever before and shit, it feels just
like breathin!

gotta get out. friends all split. pigs breathin heavy.

gotta
      get
          out

NOW!

```
    very confused now
which is good
because chaos can keep choices chooseable
structure would limit possibilities
and at every moment things have seemed
Clearly Defined
yes - new york
yes - mendocino
yes - nm
yes - san francisco
etc.
until at the typewriter i'm too busy
figuring it out
                    to get into another of my
                    Romantic Daydreams


by the way -
this was supposed to be a lovepoem to
give you on yer 18th
but i can't seem to get past the introduction
or whatever
```

"Political structures have all the appeal of a dung heap to me now."

— Jeffo

i was wondering what it is that holds people together in this fragmented society. what holds factory workers and sophisticated liberals
inside. the amerikan myth, but the amerikan myth is now specialized
to accomodate different versions for different needs. everybody's got
his own myth of society and that is what creates the society and keeps
them in it. my mind hit on a centrifuge going faster and faster until
everyone was thrown hurtling **out.** dazed, each person

stands up and looks around,
something familiar. there
son is left with only
nothing is in its
explanations, there
cause there is no
except his own body,
myths. each person
amerikan myth as his
is fragmented and de
of society for psychic
him alone, in other
into fragments, and he
whole in himself. **instead**
ated people in an all-en
fragmented, decentralized soc
sons. power to the persons?

eyes searching for
is nothing. each per-
himself. who am i?
place, there are no
is no defense be-
thing to defend
there are no
who accepts the
ticket to sanity
pends on the whole
survival. force
words rip society
will have to become
of fragmented, alien-
compassing society, a
iety of complete per-

if it's the collective myth that creates the society, why not just destroy the myths? it has become complex - there is a power elite by
fact if not conspiracy, the chains of the prisoners are attached at
the other end to the captor, exploitation for the profit of those at

the top is backed by guns. in the beginning the myth created the society.

we are not at the beginning of society and now society creates the myths, which in turn keeps it going. too many contradictions, my mind is turning to mush,but they are only contradictions in logic. we've got to destroy logic, and reason. they are foundations of bourgeois myth and power. they can be used to defeat anything, to disprove anything. they constitute a media of lies. they predict the future and repeat the past, both are definitely not true. chance and coincidence say nothing about tomorrow or yesterday, they are the media of now. lenny bruce said, "the truth is "what is," "what should be" is a dirty lie." to fight the system, we have to operate on a different plane. you know what i mean if you've ever argued logically and reasonably. win or lose, you come away knowing that you weren't getting your point across. if we want the truth, it's gotta be based on our own myth, the myth of now, and in our own language, the language of chance and spontaneous desire. logical, isn't it?

it doesn't matter if it is logical because if it is, it's purely coincidental. don't try to figure it out, and i won't explain it. the next thing after spontaneity, what logical myth-holders will try to do is get you to explain it. who's gonna pick up the garbage. don't explain it the way they want it because your answer won't make sense to

them. just pick up the nearest piece
of garbage.

that was a very long rap and   i'm sorry, but i just got carried a   way. i
originally wrote the last 3   paragraphs in three sentences but   merry
took one look at it and said   "more
rhetoric?" and i started to e   xplain
it to her and we looked at ea   ch other
and i came in here and crosse   d out
the three sentences and wrote   down my
explanation. except that i g   ot sort
of involved and rambled on.

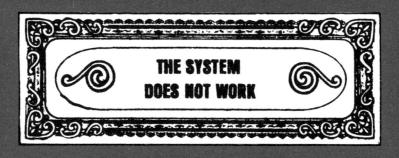

THE SYSTEM
DOES NOT WORK

it's late at night for san cristobal and we just got back from one of
those fuckin duh intellectual lefty ole discussions. and something's
been in my head for the past few weeks and this is a good chance to
lay it on y'all.

six months ago, i didn't know anyone who was dead. now i know quite a
few people and they all died of the same thing. all stabbed, poisoned,
beaten, or shot to death by amerikkka. all dead.

we sat around the kitchen table at the vincents' with john, a movement
lawyer, his two daughters, trippy & lee, trippy's mother, and craig.
john wanted to know craig's position on the weatherpeople. craig was-
n't sure; it was all a question of whether or not this is the revolution. it it isn't (and nobody seemed to know) than whetherman is
"premature."

and on. will or will not destruction of property hurt capitalism,
turn on people, affect any change. are they or are they not sincere,
should we or shouldn't we support them, do they or don't they want our
support. and on.

and all i could think was, shit! my brothers and sisters are <u>dying</u> in
this, your ideology - or theirs - won't do them any good where they are
now. they are dead or dying or running or hiding and they are further
from freedom with each siren-screaming highway. someone said he just
hoped that young people were gaining "experience" from all this stuff,
and i thought of a letter to all of us from pun i read the other day.
running, hiding...his "experience" is only bitterness and is far less
valuable to him now than the chance - oh! just one last chance! - to
share it with other people. his people. but he can't. his wife

sleeps with pain and he sleeps with his experience. and there's no turning back.

when our movement friends come through (some of our best friends are in the movement) and we talk about things and we disagree, they tell us we can't judge things right because we're so isolated. i think our isolation purifies our judgment. facts are only catalysts and knowing so few of them leaves room for what is us. i can't relate to weather-man as anything but the picture i have in my head of mark rudd on a harlem sandpile frantically looking around for someone else to take the bullhorn. i can't even begin to think about whether the time is right, or the actions. i can only try to feel inside me the reasons inside mark that led him to the cook county jail.

think about that. mark rudd standing on a harlem sandpile FRANTICALLY looking around for someone else to take the bullhorn.

WILL SOMEONE ELSE PLEASE TAKE THE BULLHORN???

no one ever thought of giving the bullhorn back to the cops, and mark rudd became a Leader. and a Symbol. and, most of all, someone you Wouldn't Want Your Daughter To Marry. and columbia shook awake and did its thing and the blacks kicked mark and ted gold and the others out of hamilton hall and told them to stay out and the term ended and columbia got a new president and went back to sleep. and mark rudd is on the run FOREVER.

and ted gold is dead.

we meet people here almost every day who tell us their names and we

know those names are **very** new and we know that we can't ask for any
others. sometimes they tell us why and sometimes they don't. but
they can never talk very much, and we feel nervous if they do. sometimes they leave the country and sometimes they try to and get busted
in the process and sometimes they dye their hair and grow a beard - or
cut one off - and try not to meet too many people. and then they get
stopped on the highway in a routine ID check and get away and resolve
that they won't go anywhere for a long, long time.

i don't know how it's going to happen. i feel that it will, that it is
at this moment happening. i don't know if bombing and rioting and
marching is adding or subtracting. i don't know if people - and there
are SO MANY of them - whose lives are shattered because of these
things feel that it's worth it. and i can't ask pun or ted gold.

i realized tonite that there's a reason for the way i feel - so strong-
ly - about weatherman and the mad bombers. we lived the way they did,
once. we worked with them and snuck into columbia to talk to them and
layed out page after page with them...and james rector died and we all
made our decisions. the only way i can judge those decisions - and
they seem to me to be almost opposite ones - is that we are living
lives as positive as seems possible in this country, and they are in
jail or dead. maybe they'll be heroes in the revolutionary history
books but i've got a better chance of being around to read them.

there's still room - at least here, at least to some extent - to avoid
being in that position. it would be easy - very easy - for us to get
into that timeless condition called fugitive. but at this moment, it's
still somewhat easy for us to stay no more outlawed than we always are.

that's something i didn't get into last night...i don't think anyone
who's had to run - for any reason - was sure, before he committed himself to that life - that it was right. i don't know, maybe that's not
true of draftdodgers and awol's but bombers and pig-shooters...i feel
that they do those things out of frustration and uncertainty. which
we feel also. but i don't take what ted and mark and marshall ended
up with lightly enough to risk it before i am sure.

but still, it affects everything we do or hope to do. that's what
stan, and craig, and the politicos tell us...you can't just do your
thing when (check one) - people are starving in (check one) india,
harlem, taos, the lower east side...repression is coming down harder
than ever...the war goes on and others begin...black capitalism is
threatening the revolution. and we answer, we will live within the
walls of their limitations and if there isn't room within them for
everyone, the walls will crack and shatter.

but sometimes, the walls move inwards like nightmares of a coney island
funhouse, much too fast and leaving no alternatives. i used to think
that you could merge living your life, farming, surviving, with invol-
ving yourself in the changes going down in the cities and the outside
world. but in a strict sense, it is impossible. sure, the mother-
fuckers hunt and farm and build kivas and dance and fuck and dope...
but their fields and forest and kiva must be abandoned at any moment,
and instantly, with no time even to bake the last loaf of bread.
they'll never be able to build a scene around themselves that is vul-
nerable to their streetfighting brothers and impenetrable by the pigs.

what really hurts is, neither will we.

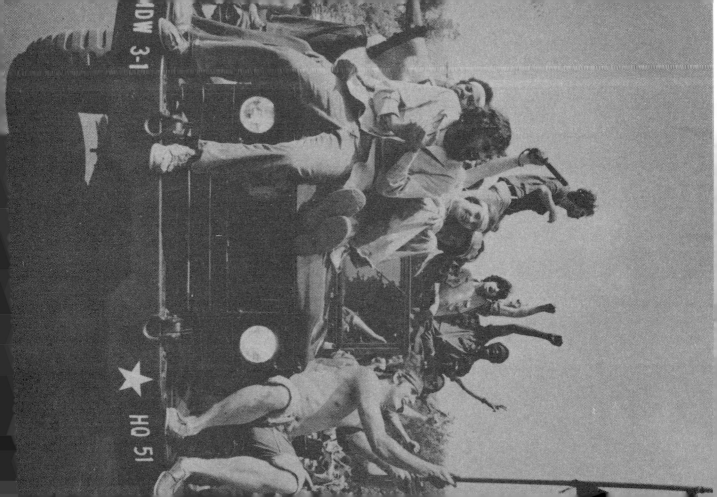

so,
comm-
une pl-
anning is
a new course
at columbia.
taught by an ex-
perienced communist.
three extra credits for
the best plan.   **'you've**
come a long way, baby.' now
i'm beginning to think of it (and the overflow crowds for ecology   at
the alternate u) as further classification and tolerance. my
first happy thought was "groovy, if they've got it in
their heads it's only one step to their bodies." now remembering the socialist sch-
olars' conference at the hilton.   office
workers for peace are office workers, not pa-
cifists. join the ranks of the Clerks' Ecology
Caucus. but, it means they want it. by next year,
they'll have courses on   women's lib, they've already got black liber   ation 237. that doesn't
mean black libera   tion is bad.   no
class can liber   ate blacks   or
create com   munes. does
it really   matter if
corpo   rations
use   en-

counter groups? does that deny anything? besides, reports are that
they're stopping them because
they can't keep non-competit-
ive sales managers. but who
gives a shit? what are we
trying to do, step on our
parents' toes? i mean,are
we trying just to piss
off the establishment
for some sort of oedi-
pal relief? or are we
trying to discover
and satisfy our de-
sires and then fight
when we're stopp-
ed? if we're not
stopped and peo-
ple still want
revenge,they
ought to real-
ize that that
is what they
want, not

enjoyment,
or social-
ism, just
revenge and
power.

i really want to write something revolutionary, but i can't think of
anything to say. d'you think it's a trend? maybe it should start with
"neon." that's always a good beginning for revolutionary raps. "neon
sagebrush." striking terror and dischord and giggles deep to the very
fart of angelfood amerika. haha. that'll do it. watch out ev'body,
the walls are crumbling. i don't know, somehow it just doesn't seem to
catch. there's too many sides. but like we got to say something revolutionary. i dig charles manson. i hate jonny weismuller. what i'd
like to start doing is writing songs. i bet i could write revolutionary songs. if someone would teach me how to make up tunes. cause i
forget them right away. i bet if lennon-mccartney helped me a little i
could write a song. hey, if anybody at columbia records is reading
this: i got a hot tip on a new super fab song writer. you could sign
me on right now for a pittance. and $50,000. see, i collect pittances.
specially prune pittances. and i collect moneys too, you oughta see my
collection. wait a minute, this isn't revolutionary. well, y'see, the
thing is, we need a goddam revolution.

merry just told me yesterday that i shouldn't say "gotta write somethin
bout this or that" and then go and write it, but i was looking through the
piles of writing on the table, and i lifted up the title page which says
"SIX - SURVIVAL PATTERNS" and there isn't anything under it. i mean like
survival can like umm be you know important, especially as far as surviving
is concerned. i've got very mixed feelings about what we should put in
here. if we really put in tricksm that means even more people are going to
come here. but they're (you're, we're) gonna come anyhow, and our loyalty's
got to be to helping our brothers and sisters stay alive. but maybe the
loyal and helpful thing to say is "don't come." nobody's going to dig this
scene when it's just another city. and there are other places to go. i
mean, what we're trying to do is show you a little of our lives, not say
taos is where it's at. but i guess the medium/message is taos no matter
what the content is. we're not about to do one of those "they did not wish
their location to be known" trips. not that this survival stuff is going
to help anyone survive, it's just a state of mind. i really think it's
important that y'all understand that this book is about us, not you, and
that we really don't think we have any answers, we just have our lives, and
we don't want the responsibility of people saying yeah i read that book and
i'm moving out there because aside from repression etc., this is our trip
and most of the time it's fun and satisfying and sometimes it's not, but
it's nothing special, it's just what we're doing. okay, now that i've done
this whole super-rationalization thing i guess everybody's going to follow
his own star anyhow so fuckit.

but what do you DO all day?!!

hi. this is much later, the book's almost done, but naturally we've left the important stuff for last. we kept saying, you know, we've got to put in something about our plans and what we're doin here and all that. i mean this book's supposed to be about our life and all there is in it are some corny wordgames and little knicknacks and excuses for not saying a fucking thing that's worth reading. and here we go again, cause the main reason i'm finally doing this is that if i don't i'll h have to do the biggest pile of dishes ever piled. and, now that i'm into it and looking for a place to begin, i can't remember what's already been said. i think that the next time we run out cē money we'll do a film.

this last winter was pretty light, but our truck kept dying so we stayed home almost all the time anyhow. usually you don't get a choice. every two weeks or so we went into town. the rest of the time went by. i really dig drawing plans and i spent a lot of time drawing dozens of houseplans and reading brochures and stuff that i was always sending for. i finally refined and drew from every angle a big one room eight-sided round house. which we're not going to build. we're going to build an A-frame. but preserving sanity during winter is a good country trick. i guess this book took up some time too. i don't really see how we could have spent six months drawing a plan and reading brochures and scribbling down this book. i did a lot of wandering. the mountains in back of our valley, especially lobo peak, are great for climbing, but i didn't climb them. i never can get any thrill our of Getting To The Top and that's a necessity when you're climbing a 12,100 mountain. so i'd rather just sit down and play with acorns. so i wandered in and out of the canyons and forest.

i don't really know what we did last winter. part of the time was passed being bored i guess, which is very bad because it leads only to periods of self-hating-pitying wakefullness and hibernat-on- like sleeps that last about 20 hours each. but we were considerably less bored once our tv finally blew its tube. of course we got it fixed yester-

day, you can't have too much of a good thing. el-
iot ness was still after lucky luciano. like i
said before, the rest of thetime went by. maybe
this give you some idea of why we haven't written
more about it. it happens, and it's fun, but now
it's past and i don't remember what it was, nor do
i particularly care. if anybody asks, just tell
em we spent the winter drinking sage tea and mumb-
ling wisely across the potbelly stove.

but how can i pretend to tell you about winter
when it's so obviously spring now. the gray is
gone from the graygreen. what was sagebrush and
chamisa only two weeks ago is now grass and little
desert flowers of the sharpest colors and strangest
blossoms. time for daisy chains in your pubic
hair. speaking of which, if i didn't already say
so, d.h. lawrence lived about a mile from here. i
did my thing for community relations the other day
which was ditch-cleaning-day. spent the day cleaning ditches. and we've been getting our garden
ready, doing the ditch, clearing the field, making
a compost heap. see, out here the water almost
never comes right out of the sky, so you need ir-
rigation ditches from the creek running in every
possible direction. and since we don't get the
kind of money they get in israel, the ditches are
slits in the ground which have to be reslitted every year. from what i've gathered, this land was
once much greener, which is not to say that it was
ever any good for rice paddies, but i'll tell you
a little ecologicky story. once it was all fores-
ted. the forests were cut down for cattle. the
wolves and coyotes were killed cause they got the
cattle. the rabbits and rodents took over cause
there weren't no wolves and coyotes. by then the
grass was mostly gone, so the sheep were brought in
cause they eat the roots of the grass and stamp
the rest into the ground with their hooves. and
the rabbits and rodents destroyed what was left.
so when the snow melted, instead of seeping into
the soil, the water ran off in flash floods. now,
except for little valleys like this, it's a desert.
the grasslands and forests are gone. there's
still enough left to feed yourself, but no one
does that, even in this valley. and they're cut-
ting down what's left of the forest for more graz-
ing land. but there's a lot of people out here
now who want to work with the land, not do anything
to it, so maybe it'll work out. if you're pissed,
write yer rep in the capitol, he just voted for the
latest earth death bill.

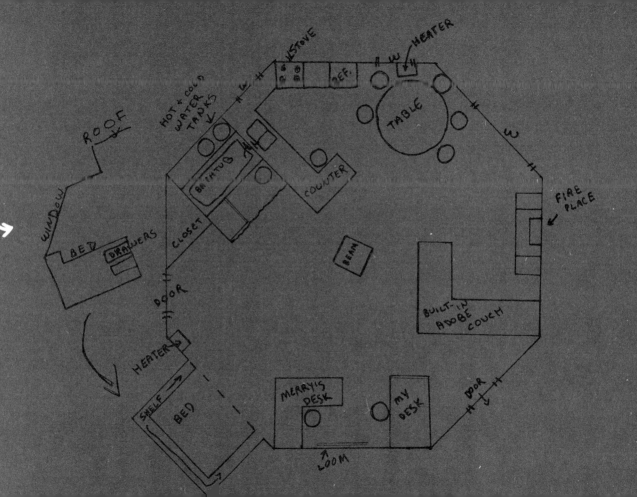

THE ORIGINAL & FUTURE PLAN

ROOF

WINDOW

BED

DRAWERS

HOT + COLD WATER TANKS

BATHTUB

CLOSET

DOOR

HEATER

SHELF

BED

STOVE

REF.

HEATER

TABLE

COUNTER

BEAM

FIRE PLACE

BUILT-IN ADOBE COUCH

MERRY'S DESK

MY DESK

DOOR

LOOM

VIEW FROM THE TOP OF ORIGINAL PLAN

THE LATER & PRESENT
PLAN

AND THEN....

WE STARTED LOOKING FOR LAND....

we both agree, there really has to be something about "all this" in the book. it's just so fucking hard to write about. if you were here and not sitting there reading this, maybe i could tell you. but maybe not. it's hard even to think about.

how do you describe in words, trying to put all of your energy into belief in magic & joy, into people and land, into concepts and adobe, and feeling suddenly that you just don't have enough energy to main- tain that faith? how do you write about hitting upon something, an idea, yes, but something that could be (and was and is still) real - something that seems to be the culmination of all that 2 people have been and want to be - and watching its possibility fade? i cannot de- scribe to you or make you feel, really, what it has been like for us these past few months.

our desires were (and are, by unimpared standards) simple. we thought the hardest part was recognizing them. that's what all our rhetoric used to say. we wanted some land. not much. we wanted to build, ourselves with loving help, a home. we wanted a child or more and a horse and a place for cicero to grow younger gracefully and a place for willie to hunt and room for a few chicken coops and a few people we might find or refind some day.

in paul's words, we wanted a base. we wanted a place to sit and watch it all happen from, to make our decisions with. we are not marching or organizing or bombing buildings because we are not sure. we feel a need to be sure of ourselves, first. we wanted a reality in our lives from which we could live out the days and weeks and maybe even years we and the world have left to smile.

so, we started looking for land. first, the ranch. we picked out 3
homesites and showed them to craig. they were all beautiful. craig
wasn't sure about his plans for his land. and people were coming over
for baths all the time and feeling the need to talk first and later,
and laying their heavy raps on us & making us decide that san cristobal was too tight and close. craig still wasn't sure. so we called
some real estate agents. 20 acres or so, we told them, isolated and
around $10,000. we found a place near lama, the most beautiful area
in this part of the planet. we brought elizabeth, our waterwitch, up
& she found a spot for a well. paul wrote beautiful words about it &
i learned to love it. then we tried to get the money for it.

paul's mother wouldn't let go of his trust fund. college, she said.
college? i sat in the other room knowing that if the phone call was
taking this long the answer was no. i decided to call my parents. my
mother said probly yes, call back tomorrow for details. the next day,
my father said no. i can't write about the anguish. can you imagine
it? we started haggling about paying on time, hating the idea but not
knowing what else to do. car loans. $150 a month just for debts.
could this be us?

we tried avoiding the real estate people. finally we called them &
found out we'd been looking at the wrong piece of land. the surveyor
had discovered it was something else. we looked at what he told us
was it. it was about 15 acres of pinyon & canyon & 5 acres of culti-
vated, irrigated land. who'd done the plowing? must have been a
neighbor, farming land unused for 30 years. a miracle. i was afraid
to fall in love with it. i prayed for my pessimism to be unreal. irrigated land for $7500? we decided not to mention the water to any-
one. but still...no money.

i freaked & wrote to my parents. i can't tell you about that letter
either. about a week later, got 3 telegrams one day to call immediat-
ely. quaking, called. "we've decided to buy you the land, meredith."
and what can i say about what we felt then?

the next day we went up to the land to plan where things would go. the
man from the nearest house came over. "was it you who plowed this
land, pete?" "of course i did, it's my land. i told those people a
year ago their land is down there."

we looked at it and knew we didn't want it. went to the real estate
people & everyone brought in their deeds and sure enough, pete owned
the piece we wanted. wouldn't sell. we were landless...again.

we thought about europe. or maybe another planet? where is there
room left for us? but we'd have to leave willie & cicero not to mention several thousand dreams. so we started looking again. it's
april. can't start building later than june. we've been looking
further & further from where we want to be. we've begun thinking of
compromise & forgetting magic. maybe vermont. vermont?

this has none of it in it. but it's all i can give you. i've done
what we said we had to do, write something about "all this." you know
the facts. does it do anything to your mind, your body? i want you
to understand, but not badly enough to open myself up to all the pain
that waits like a dagger dripping with blood. not enough to try to
make you feel what it's like to try so hard to let it flow and have it
all dammed at every breath. not enough to go any further than right
...here.

laterwords: we've completed the cycle. craig's decided to part with
the first piece of land we wanted, above the ranch; there's a well
there and possible hook-up with the community water system being set
up now. the only person who's ever lived there is the same guy who
once lived in the first house we lived in in san cristobal. the remains
of his house have tumbled into the rosehip patch and remind us that
nothing is more permanent than we can make it. we leave this house,
with its closets and walls and doors and sears' best bathtub for...
what? for tomorrow and hopes of a better history yet to come.
wish us luck!!!

M'MIND HUFFIN'-PUFFIN' AWAY JUST

NOTHER DREAM. AIN'T IT THE FUCKIN TRUTH. GOT THAT OL MAGIC WORKIN TONITE
AND CAN'T LET GO OF IT OR IT OF ME. ENERGY FLOWS THRU THE PHONE, MOST UN-
USUAL, ENERGYFLOWS ALWAYS MOST UNUSUAL EVERY DAY. JUST NOTHER DREAM IS
LIFE. THAT'S ALL THERE IS AND IT'S ALL THERE. SURFIN AND SLIDIN THRU
MOUNTAIN-MESA TIMES AND WHATEVER GAME YER PLAYIN' MY MAN, DON'T WORRY, DO
NOT WORRY, IT'S JUST ANOTHER DREAM, BELIEVIN IN THE POWER OF A MILLION SUNS
- WHO CN DENY IT? - PAINTING THIS PAPER AND EVEN A BOOK FULL OF WORDS, DO
YOU HAVE ANY IDEA HOW MANY WORDS ARE AVAILABLE DOES IT PAINT A PICTURE, OR
DOES IT JUST PAINT WORDS, THIS MACHINE'S A WORD ARTIST AND IT'S GOT MORE
COMBINATIONS THAN I COULD TELL YOU ABOUT. AND IF IT DON'T WORK OUT, JUST
THROW IN ANOTHER PHOTO. WHAT'S IN HERE'S ONLY IMPORTANT T US AN YOU, THE
MESSAGE IS JUST THAT SOMETHIN'S HAPPENIN IN THIS OL WORLD. WHAT CN WE TELL
YOU ABOUT THAT? SEE, MY NAME'S PAUL, HOW DO YOU DO, BUT I KNOW YOUR NAME'S
NOT IBM RENTAL, SO WHAT CAN I TELL YOU? DO YOU REALIZE THAT THESE ARE JUST
SYMBOLS ON A PIECE OF PAPER AND THAT IF I SHOW IT T MY DOG HE WON'T EVEN
EAT IT OR PISS ON IT. VERY MEANINGLESS, GET OUT YER FINGERPAINTS.

M'MIND HUFFIN-PUFFIN' AWAY JUST

LIFE. THAT'S ALL THERE IS AND IT'S ALL THERE. SURPRIN AND SLIDIN THRU
MOUNTAIN-MESA TIMES AND WHATEVER GAME YER PLAYIN' MY MAN. DON'T WORRY, DO
YOU HAVE ANY IDEA HOW MANY WORDS ARE AVAILABLE DOES IT PAINT A PICTURE, OR
COMBINATIONS THAN I COULD TELL YOU ABOUT. AND IF IT DON'T WORK OUT, JUST
THROW IN ANOTHER PHOTO. WHAT'S IN HERE'Z ONLY IMPORTANT T'US AN YOU, THE
YOU ABOUT THAT. SEE, MY NAME'Z PAUL. HOW DO YOU DO, BUT I KNOW YOUR NAME'Z

when we went
to new york to get
the contract for this
book, we spent a lot of time
seeing publishers. right on.one
cat, the editor for our other book, sat behind a bigger (but still
plastic) desk than the last time we
saw him. his hair was longer, his pin-
stripe bell-bottom suit had a sharper
crease, and like that. we told him what
we were doing in the city and probly o-
ther stuff. he told us that if we were
writing a book about what we were doing,
we didn't have it together. the truth is
that we are so together we've gone one
circle higher on the spiral and trans-
cended that logic. the truth is that
winter's cold and we had to pay
the gas and rent. the truth is
that we are not together. the
truth is that there is
no truth, that
there

is no
together,
that we're
just playing
a different
game.

right
on!

spend my time sitting on a fence
whistling at the sun,
and playing with the ants
humming my song that don't make sense
saving the world in my brand new pants

```
lovelovelovelovelovelovelovelovelovelovelovelovelovelovelovelove
lovelovelovelovelovelovelovelovelovelovelovelovelovelovelovelove
lovelovelovelovelovelovelovelovelovelovelovelovelovelovelovelove
lovelovelovelovelovelovelovelovelovelovelovelovelovelovelovelove
lovelovelovelovelovelovelovelovelovelovelovelovelovelovelovelove
lovelovelovelovelovelovelovelovelovelovelovelovelovelovelovelove
love      lovelovelove        elovel    ovelov      elo          elove
love      lovelovelov             lovelo    velo      velo         elove
love      lovelovelov      e      lovelo    velo      velo  lovelovelove
love      lovelovelo      vel     ovelov    el      ovelo  lovelovelove
love      lovelovelo      vel     ovelov    el      ovelo      lovelove
love      lovelovelov      e     lovelove    1     lovelo      lovelove
love      lovelovelov           lovelove          lovelo  lovelovelove
love         velov             lovelove          lovelo  lovelovelove
love         velove            lovelove          lovelo      lovelove
love         velovel          elovelovel      elovelo        lovelove
love         velovel          velovelovelo    velovelo       lovelove
love         velovelo        ovelovelovelov   ovelovelo       lovelove
lovelovelovelovelovelovelovelovelovelovelovelovelovelovelovelove
lovelovelovelovelovelovelovelovelovelovelovelovelovelovelovelove
lovelovelovelovelovelovelovelovelovelovelovelovelovelovelovelove
lovelovelovelovelovelovelovelovelovelovelovelovelovelovelovelove
lovelovelovelovelovelovelovelovelovelovelovelovelovelovelovelove
lovelovelovelovelovelovelovelovelovelovelovelovelovelovelovelove
```

some
times
sun don shine

sometimes it
taste like wine

'times
ain't no rhyme

some
times
gravity
seems
to stop
for
all time.

the time was, not so long ago, a pippsee name of ceg, calling himself
as keg, was found overjoyously parading past wheyman's drug store without any clothes on. in those ears they were proney to calling it many
gorilla theater and the price of admission was held down by it.
a mind gasped its last gas in those dates.

HEY, YOU! you're what's known as a captive audience. you are reading these words and i wrote them for that reason. trapped!!

you are, first, paul. and then, maybe, trippy or lee or jason epstein or a lawyer at random house. i am talking to YOU. *now to think of something to say...*

the game is exposed. the things i would write on this page, then retype and paste on a layout sheet, are not the things i would write to, or tell, jason epstein or maybe even trippy and lee. yet i have written those things and will write more of them and jason and trippy and lee and my parents and many others will know them about me. secrets won't be secrets any more. if this book is going to be revolutionary, or even unique, it will be only because i will write these things, let you share my privacy, without the guise of Characters and a Plot. no critic will have the privilege of guessing which character is me and which is trippy, which thought expressed in quotation marks are really paul's or lee's.

and i'm trying to break on through to the other side. this is a piece of paper with some thoughts on it and maybe soon it will be a page, a part, of a book. will the thoughts have more value to you, or to me, because they are printed instead of typed?

can this be? when we talk about it and begin to lay it out, i can only look for a rhythm, a pace maintained and as much honesty as possible. the same thing i seek in a day. YOU - please realize that we are real, we are doing nothing that sets us apart from you any more than a smile or a tear. we are special in our own way the way you are in yours.

hasta la vista, compadres.

HERE IT IS!
the next Startling
Episode in the Continuing
Story of the Salvation of
the World! our last circumstance
left the Hero and his Charming
Bride bidding a Sorrowed Hesitance
to the Travel Plans of their Hip Com-
panions. but, things have Changed. Ho
Chi Minh died today. Boredom threatens.
This break-out will be prophesied. Dol-
drums attack the Creative (hexagram one
will prevail). The discovery of the next
medium. The need for re-naissance. My hor-
ny self & yours to be acknowledged. The
Show Must Go On. The massage transformed
again to the message. It must be the
burst of the sun.

Today. Tomorrow streaks - flash of
mountain Dawn recharging. No
more broken patterns by the
sun sitting and digging
maybe you. Reason
greasin'&

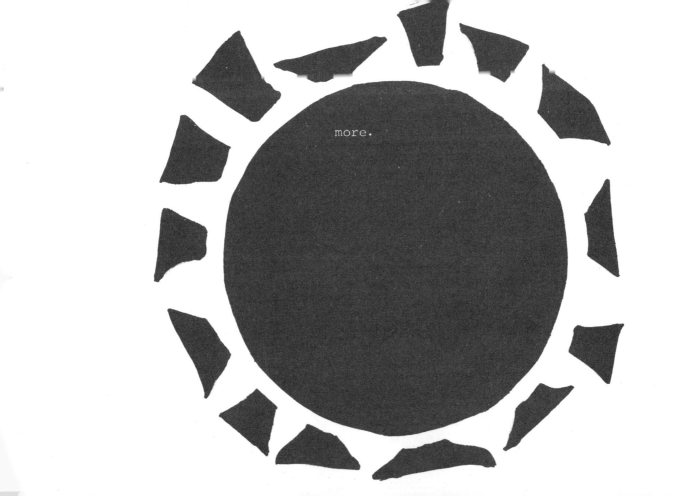

more.

Paul and Meredith live in a one-room house they built themselves in
Taos, New Mexico. Before that, they were students at the Bronx High
School of Science, an elite school in New York City for intellectually
gifted children. There Paul began one of the first underground
high school newspapers, printing it on the school's mimeo machine.
For this action and others like it, he was subsequently expelled.
He and Meredith took an apartment together in the Village and
joined the underground newspaper RAT. Like other radicals,
they might have stayed in N.Y.C., worked for RAT, gone to Chicago
in '68, and continued the direct attack on the values with
which they found they could not live. But instead, they dropped
out even further and left for Taos, New Mexico.